FASTBACK® Mystery

The Face That Stopped Time

MEL CEBULASH

GLOBE FEARON
Pearson Learning Group

FASTBACK® MYSTERY BOOKS

Bill Waite's Will	The Good Luck Smiling Cat
Cardiac Arrest	The Intruder
Dawson's City	Janie
The Diary	Meeting at Joe's
The Face That Stopped Time	No Witnesses
A Game for Fools	Suspicion

All photography © Pearson Education, Inc. (PEI) unless specifically noted.

Copyright © 2004 by Pearson Education, Inc., publishing as Globe Fearon®, an imprint of Pearson Learning Group, 299 Jefferson Road, Parsippany, NJ 07054. All rights reserved. No part of this book may be reproduced or transmitted in any form or by any means, electronic or mechanical, including photocopying, recording, or by any information storage and retrieval system, without permission in writing from the publisher. For information regarding permission(s), write to Rights and Permissions Department.

Globe Fearon® and Fastback® are registered trademarks of Globe Fearon, Inc.

ISBN 0-13-024541-0
Printed in the United States of America
1 2 3 4 5 6 7 8 9 10   07 06 05 04 03

1-800-321-3106
www.pearsonlearning.com

The shooting was a terrible mistake. That fact was written all over George Hawkins's wrinkled old face. He had shot a young woman who had entered his house. She was dead, and he was sorry. Detective Paul Suriano could tell that. Still, the whole thing didn't make much sense.

The young woman, Lorraine Smith, had been a reporter at the local newspaper. Why she had decided to walk into George Hawkins's house was a mystery. Hawkins had heard someone on the porch, taken up his rifle, and fired as soon as the woman had entered the house. It wasn't a bright thing to do, but he was an old man. And as he explained, he was frightened. He was going to be booked on a murder charge, but he would probably get off. After all, old people had a right to protect themselves.

Before Hawkins was taken to the police station, Detective Suriano learned what he could about the man. Hawkins had lived in the house in North Bergen for about 20 years. Before that, he had lived in Cliffside Park, a nearby town. He had worked at a factory in Edgewater for nearly 30 years. Two years ago, Hawkins had retired from his factory job. He said that he had never seen Lorraine Smith before she walked into his house.

The shooting bothered Paul Suriano. All his murder cases did, of course, but this one had some odd things about it. Hawkins seemed innocent enough. Lorraine Smith had been a reporter—did she want to interview Hawkins about something? Surely she would have called him first. Why did he shoot her?

The next morning Suriano visited the newspaper office and interviewed four editors. None of them had any idea why Miss Smith had gone to Hawkins's house. They all wanted to help, but they really had nothing to tell.

A call on Miss Smith's parents provided no help for Paul Suriano either. They were quite upset and even angry at Hawkins, but they didn't know the man. And they couldn't think of any reason why their daughter would have entered his house.

"Do you suspect that this Hawkins planned to kill my daughter?" Mr. Smith asked.

"No," Suriano answered. "It seems as if he was just frightened. I'm only making a routine check. We may never find out why your daughter walked in on the old man."

"We have to find out," Mr. Smith said. "Something's wrong about this, and you know it. I'm no fool."

"I'll do what I can," Suriano promised. "You and your wife just take care of yourselves."

As Paul Suriano drove off, the picture of Lorraine Smith's dead body came back into his mind. He realized that she had looked a little like her father. Suriano couldn't blame the man or his wife for being angry at Hawkins, even if the old man was no longer mentally competent. They deserved to know some reason for their daughter's deadly mistake. If there was a reason, he was going to find it.

Suriano's next stop was the factory in Edgewater where Hawkins had worked for most of his life. Suriano found the factory supervisor.

"Of course, I remember Hawkins," the supervisor said. "He was good at his job, but he was a bitter man. People said that he changed after the death of his son. That was years ago, before my time here. He lost his wife around six years ago. I've heard that the son took his own life, but I don't know that for sure." Suriano's mind leaped to the death of the reporter, but he saw no logical connection. He was hanging on a small thread of information. Still, it was the only thread Suriano had found. He could ask Hawkins about his son. Or he could find out for himself. He finally decided against asking Hawkins. Right now, there was no sense in bringing up bad memories for the old man. Hawkins already had enough to think about.

The next morning Paul Suriano traveled to Cliffside Park to see Chief Myers. Ralph Myers was about Hawkins's age and had been on the Cliffside Park police force most of his life. If there was something strange about the death of Hawkins's son. Myers would know.

"I heard about that shooting you had," Myers said, shaking his head. "Funny that George Hawkins shot a reporter. It kind of reminds me of the Terry Hawkins case."

Suriano slid forward on his seat. "What do you mean?" he asked.

"I wouldn't make too much of it," Myers began. "After all, the Terry Hawkins thing is very old news—about 25 years old. Terry was the old man's son. He jumped from the roof of the newspaper building. Either he didn't like his job much or it was the easiest place to jump from."

"Was he killed?" Suriano asked.

"Sure was," Myers replied. "It's quite a long drop from that roof to the street." Myers looked across at Suriano. "I guess there were a lot of things bothering the kid," he went on. "He didn't leave a note or anything, but his old man blamed the newspaper. He said everyone picked on Terry." Myers shrugged. "Maybe they did."

"Did anyone check on that?" Suriano asked.

"I never found out," Myers said. "We know the kid's death wasn't murder. A lot of people saw him alone on the roof. They called to him, and people raced up there, but it was too late. I guess his mind was made up. He jumped without a word of warning. The whole town was shocked. In fact, I think the door to that roof is still locked."

"Well, I can't blame Hawkins for being upset," Suriano said. "This Terry was his only kid."

"Yeah," Myers grunted, "but you don't think the shooting of that reporter has anything to do with Terry's death, do you? From what I read, the whole thing was a sad accident. I'd like to know though what she was doing at Hawkins's place. Have you figured that out yet?"

"That's the problem," Suriano said, frowning. "It doesn't make any sense that I can see."

Myers smiled. "A lot of things don't make sense in this business we're in. Sometimes the accidents are as stupid as the crimes."

"That's true," Suriano said, "but I'm going to dig a little more. I wonder whether anyone who worked with Terry Hawkins is still at the paper."

"I imagine so," Myers said. "Maureen

Markel, the secretary over there, would know. She's older than I am."

"Well, I think I'll try talking to her," Suriano said. He got up from his seat and held out his hand. "Thanks for the information," he said. "I'm probably wasting my time, but I guess we get paid for that, too."

"Yeah, I guess so," Myers said. "In another year or so, I'll be getting paid to stay at home and mow my lawn. The funny thing is that I'm not going to like it any more than the taxpayers will."

Suriano looked into the chief's face and smiled at the old man. "I know what you mean," he told Myers. "I wouldn't care for that either."

"Let me know what you turn up," Myers said as Suriano went out the door.

There were at least a dozen people working in the front office of the *Times-Herald*, but Suriano didn't have any trouble spotting Maureen Markel. She was definitely the oldest person in the office.

Suriano introduced himself. Then he said, "I wish you would answer a few questions for me."

"I wish you'd ask them," she replied. "This is a busy place."

"Do you remember Terry Hawkins?" Suriano shot back.

"Of course, I remember," she said. "Everyone is talking about his father shooting our Lorraine."

"Is anyone who worked with him still here?"

Maureen Markel looked into the distance. "Let me think," she said. "Mr. Vath was one of Terry's editors. He's still here. And Mrs. Peterson was an intern. She's still here, too. That's all, I think. Mr. Vath is in his office. I'm sure he'd talk to you. Now let me ask you a question."

"Go ahead," Suriano said.

"Why are you asking about Terry Hawkins now? Is there a connection to Lorraine, do you think?"

"I don't have an answer," Suriano told her. "Old cases come up sometimes in the course of my work. When this one did, I decided to check out some facts."

"I don't think the facts have changed," she said sadly. "Well, I'll see whether Mr. Vath is free. I have work to do."

Suriano waited in the reception area for

only a few minutes. The man who came through the door looked close to retirement age.

"I'd like to ask you a few questions about Terry Hawkins," Suriano told him. "I know it's been a long time, but I think you may be able to help me. What do you remember about Terry?"

Mr. Vath gazed out the window. "I remember him as shy," he said slowly. "He didn't have many friends, and he probably wasn't cut out for the news business. I tried to push him to do more interviews, track down more sources, but it didn't do much good. I think he would have been happier with a desk job than one that meant going out and talking with people. I felt pretty bad about what happened. I suppose I felt as if I could have helped him, but to this day, I still don't know how. No one ever suspected he would do what he did."

"I'm sure," Suriano said. "How did his family take it?"

"How do you imagine?" Vath replied, not expecting an answer. "They were upset. The father blamed it on Terry's supervisors. I guess he included me in that. He was angry and maybe even felt a little guilty himself. Some of the staff seemed to think that Terry didn't get along with his father. When things like that happen, some of us look inside ourselves, and others look for someone else to blame. If I had been Terry's father, I don't know what I would have done. The mother was all broken up. You could see it at the funeral. But she wasn't mad. She was just hurt."

"Thank you," Suriano said. "This has been helpful. Can you tell me where to find Mrs. Peterson?"

"I'll take you," the editor said, lifting his rugged-looking body up from the chair. "Of course we ran a story about Hawkins shooting one of our reporters. I know that's what brings you here. But does it have anything to do with something that happened 25 years ago?"

"It probably doesn't," Suriano said. "I'm just making sure."

Mrs. Peterson was a tall dark-haired woman. Suriano guessed that she must have been a very young reporter 20 years earlier. While Suriano talked to her, she kept glancing at her computer monitor as though she wanted the conversation to be over quickly.

"I remember Terry quite well," she said. "He and I both worked for Mary Ritter. We were both just starting out in the news business. He had been hired as a reporter for the local news. I was a summer intern. Mary kept us both very busy. Terry was almost a project for her. She was sure that she could make him into a good reporter. But I never believed Mary was his reason for jumping."

Suriano's face showed his surprise.

"I'm sorry," Mrs. Peterson said, "but you have to understand that Terry's father was so awful about the whole thing that I never got over it. I suppose you know that he blamed us. That wasn't fair of him."

"There's no telling how anyone would act in the same situation," Suriano said. "Later, he may have been sorry he blamed anyone."

"I'd like to think so," said Mrs. Peterson, "but, honestly, I doubt it. There was something mean about that man. I could see it in his eyes at the funeral. He seemed more angry than sad."

Then she asked the question Suriano had been hearing all day: "You don't think there's any connection between Terry's death and Lorraine's do you?"

"It doesn't seem likely," Suriano said. "Is anyone else Terry knew still here?"

Mrs. Peterson thought for a while. "No," she finally answered. "Mr. Vath and I are the only ones left. Mr. Warren retired to Maine, and Mary Ritter left the paper a few years ago. She lives in North Bergen. On 79th Street, I think."

Suriano wrote down the information about Mary Ritter. Then he thanked Mrs. Peterson.

Stopping at a phone booth on the way back to North Bergen, Suriano found the number and address of the Ritter family on 79th Street. After that, he parked by a coffee shop near the North Bergen city line and went inside. He needed to think about what he had learned and decide whether he really needed to see Mrs. Ritter. He supposed that she would have much the same story to tell about the sad life of Terry Hawkins. If the boy's death had anything to do with the death of Lorraine Smith, it was going to be a surprise to Suriano.

Suriano had read enough newspaper articles about the health dangers of coffee to fill a small book. Still, the tired detective enjoyed the three cups he drank. He left the shop with new energy and headed for the address he had found for Mary Ritter. He didn't expect to learn much from her, but her home was near the station. There was no sense in passing it by.

The Ritters lived in a one-family, brick, ranch-style house with a driveway on the side. The nice house and the new Cadillac parked in the driveway seemed to show that the Ritters had some money. Suriano pressed the doorbell and heard the chimes ringing inside. There was no answer. After a few moments, Suriano rang again.

This time he could hear yelping coming from a room toward the back of the house. "Can I help?" a voice asked.

He turned and saw a young man coming up the walk to the front door.

"I don't know," Suriano said. "I'm looking for Mary Ritter."

"She's my mom," the young man explained. "Who are you?"

Suriano showed his badge for the first time that day. "I want to talk to her about someone who used to work at the *Times-Herald*," he said.

"Mom and Dad have been out of town for a couple of weeks," the young man said. "I'm watching the house for them and feeding the dogs. They'll be back in two days. I hope you can wait that long. I can give you her cell phone number."

"Thanks, I'd appreciate it," said Soriano. "I may not call her right away. This particular matter isn't urgent."

He jotted down the number and walked back to his car. As he opened the door, he could hear behind him the excited greeting the young man was getting from his parents' dogs.

I said it wasn't urgent, he thought. I've told three people that there's probably no connection between Terry Hawkins and Lorraine Smith. But the longer I think about this, the more I wonder.

Back at the station, Suriano ran into Nick Davis. Davis was Suriano's partner.

"Where have you been hiding?" Davis joked.

"I've been doing a little checking on the Hawkins case," Suriano explained. "Something about it bothers me."

"Something about it bothers a lot of people," Davis said. "The old guy is out on bail, and the woman's family is beginning to ask questions. In their place, I'd be asking questions, too. They don't think she would have gone to Hawkins's house if someone hadn't sent her or invited her. I tend to agree with them. We know she wasn't on a story assignment for the paper. Proving the old man was waiting for her would be hard. In the first place, we don't have a motive. What did you find out?"

"Some interesting things," Suriano replied. He told Davis all the facts he had.

When Suriano finished, Davis shook his head. "It's interesting," he said, "but I still can't make the connection. Why would the old man want to kill that reporter? Do you think he would have killed anyone from the paper because of what happened to his son?"

Suriano frowned. "If that's the case, he sure took a long time getting around to it," he said. "And why Lorraine Smith? To be honest, I don't know what to think. Did you talk to the old man? What did you think of him?"

"I think he's a little crazy," Davis said. "He has that look in his eyes. You know the look. I see it around here sometimes."

Suriano laughed. "Yeah, I know the look, but I guess I wouldn't be surprised to see it on the face of a guy who shoots first and says 'Who's there?' later."

Suriano's desk was piled high with reports and junk mail. He threw the junk mail away without opening it. Then he sat down with a cup of coffee to look over the reports. Several cases needed looking into. He was behind on his work, and he knew he would have to push the Lorraine Smith case out of his mind for a few days.

Three days later something happened to remind Suriano about old Hawkins. A funeral notice for Lorraine Smith caught his attention when he was going through the morning paper. "Friends and relatives are invited,"

Suriano read. The words made him feel sorry once again for the young woman and her family. The question marks about her death needed to be cleared up.

Suriano thought about calling Mary Ritter. She and her husband were probably back from their trip. He guessed that they had been on vacation. He wondered what her husband did for a living. They had money. There was no doubt about that. He remembered the big Cadillac parked in their driveway. He could see it in his mind. It wasn't a rented car. It was their car. He knew that from—

Suddenly, Suriano was struck with an idea. "Hey, Nick," he called to his partner, who was sitting at the other desk in their office. "I just got an idea. It's a wild one, but if I'm right, we may want to talk to

Hawkins. If I call you, can you bring him in?"

"Sure," Davis said. "But why don't you let me in on your wild idea. I don't want to bother the old guy if we really don't have to."

By the time Suriano finished explaining, Nick Davis was smiling. "Now wouldn't that be wild!" Davis said. "I imagine the odds against your hunch are a million to one. But I've heard of stranger things. You know you could save a lot of time by calling."

"I know," Suriano agreed. "But if I'm only partly right, I'm going to need a few other answers. And I suppose we'll need Mrs. Ritter."

Several hours later, North Bergen's chief of police found himself smiling at

Detectives Suriano and Davis. "I just heard that you have the old guy locked up again," the chief said. "I hear he planned the whole thing and now he's admitted it. How did you two get him to change his mind about talking?"

"You tell him, Paul," Davis said. "It was your wild idea."

Starting at the beginning, Suriano went over the case. Then he described how the sight of Mrs. Ritter had suddenly made the old man upset enough to talk.

"Let's see if I follow all of this," the chief said. "Mrs. Ritter was Miss Smith at the *Times-Herald* when Hawkins's son died. After almost 25 years, Hawkins happens to see Mrs. Ritter while he's shopping at the North Bergen Mall. He remembers her face, even though she is a lot older. Her face stops time for him, and he goes back in his mind to the time of his son's death. He figures that she's still working at the newspaper, and he calls there for Miss Smith. Lorraine Smith gets the call. He must have made up some story about needing to talk to her about his son. She goes to visit him, and he's waiting with the rifle. When she walks through the door, he kills her. Then he comes to his senses and sees that she's the wrong person."

"You got it," Suriano said. "As soon as he saw Mary Ritter today, he went to pieces. He knows that he was wrong to do what he did, and I think he's really sorry. It's just too bad that he didn't look before he fired. He's a sad old man and probably a pretty sick one, too."

"There's just one little problem with all

this," the chief said. "How did you figure out that Mary Ritter was once Mary Smith?"

"You're not going to believe this," Suriano said, grinning at his partner. "It was the license plate on the big Cadillac. That did it. When I first went to the Ritter house, I looked at the license plate, the way I look at all plates. The Ritters have one of those husband-wife initial plates. The initials were MSR-RWR. I didn't think much of it at the time. But then today, I remembered the plate. I figured that if MSR stood for Mary S. Ritter, the S might stand for Smith. And I was right."

The chief smiled at his two detectives. "A thousand-to-one shot," he said with pleasure, "but good work."

"Yeah," Davis said, grinning at him.

"But I figured the odds were a million-to-one, Chief. Let's be fair."

The chief laughed first, but Suriano and Davis quickly joined in.

Other cases were still open. But the case of the Lorraine Smith murder was closed, and Paul Suriano felt good.